Love Won, Love Lost, Love Longed For

Love is won by those brave enough to keep their hearts in the race!
Love is lost by those too selfish to share their space!
Love is longed for by those who had it and let it slip away!

Verna Buchanan

authorHOUSE®

AuthorHouse™
1663 Liberty Drive
Bloomington, IN 47403
www.authorhouse.com
Phone: 1-800-839-8640

Published by AuthorHouse   12/18/2014

ISBN: 978-1-4969-5393-3 (sc)
ISBN: 978-1-4969-5392-6 (e)

This book is dedicated to my Family.

Whose love no yardstick could ever measure.
While this book of poetry speaks of the many facets of love I am always overwhelmed by my family's love!

This book is dedicated to my Manager, Rosemary. Every day I try to apply the Rosemary Theory to my life.

This book is dedicated to all of the lovers in this world. This book is dedicated to all of those still searching and to those who are smart enough to know that they have found it!

This book is dedicated to the calming soul who listens to me and tries to help me figure out this maze called life.

So many words in my head.
So many things still to be said.
I am a work in progress
and you have not read the best of me yet!

This is Verna Buchanan's 2nd published book.

To Verna

Verna, thank you for letting us take this journey with you. May the world now know your God given gift of words. Not many have the ability to drop such eloquent profound words in the flicker of a moment.

You exude words like others breathe. We still marvel at your talent. We all want to thank you for sharing with us.

A reviewer wrote about Verna Buchanan's first published book *Save Us, Save The World, a Cry From the Children* on <u>www.goodreads.com</u> the *following*:

"These are poems that come from experience, the heart, understanding, compassion and wisdom. You will come to know Verna Buchanan from reading them and you will be a more complete person."

After reading this book go to <u>www.goodreads.com</u> review and rate.

If you bought from Amazon.com leave a review there also.

LOVE WON
LOVE LOST
LOVE LONGED FOR

Written By
Verna Buchanan

youneedwords.com
verna@youneedwords.com

youtube.com/youneedwords

Listen to lyrics like:

- I'm So Blessed
- Meet Me in Memphis
- Curtains Blowing in the Breeze
- You Need Words
- Every Man Likes A Little Crazy In A Woman
- God I Appreciate You
- Bible Belt Blues

You Need Words
Chicago, IL North Little Rock, AR

Contents

Chapter 1: LOVE WON

Chapter 2: LOVE LOST

Chapter 3: LOVE LONGED FOR

Chapter 1
LOVE WON

Love, Life's Greatest Mystery

Life's greatest mystery is love.
Something scholars can't explain.
They know why no matter how you divide
2 by 2 it still comes out the same
but nobody knows why I enjoy
walking with you in the rain.

Life's greatest mystery is love.
Einstein with all of his knowledge,
Pharaoh with all of his gold,
neither one could figure out why love has such control.
Read about it in books and fall into it with just one look.

Life's greatest mystery is love.
Love has torn down empires.
Love has brought kings and queens to their knees.
Love has taken the strongest of men and women
and left them talking to themselves and wandering aimlessly in the
streets.

Life's greatest mystery is love.
Something scientist can't figure out
no matter how much they explore.
They know why the night turns to day, but
nobody knows why you make me feel this way.

Just A Poem To Say I Love You

I don't know any sad songs.
I can't remember the last time I shed a tear.
I have no reasons for unhappiness since you
and your love stopped here.
I can't join in on conversations about low down dirty men.
I can't relate to that kind of thing since
you opened up your world and let me in.

I wake up in the mornings with a smile on my face.
I turn to you and I know that your arms are the safest place.
I go through my day-to-day routine walking on air because I know
that when my day is over your love will be there.
I anticipate the touch of you with every fiber in my body.
I long for the manly scent of you all through the day.
I smile to myself on the street and rush on my way
because each hour brings me closer to the end of another day and
closer to you.

I will unlock the door to a house that is full of love.
Whether we spend the evening with friends or alone,
the time will be well spent and we will make
this love grow strong.
I don't watch the soap operas.
There is too much breaking up, packing up and moving out.
My life is a fairytale with you,
not a daytime drama for Channel 2.
Just a poem to say I love you.

I Am In Your Corner

When everything around you is crumbling,
when your life is in turmoil,
when your confidence is tumbling,
when you seem to sink lower with every move you make,
when you think you can't win with every step you take,
when you think it isn't worth the fight,
when you think that nobody understands,
baby don't despair, don't you quit, don't you do it.
I will reach across oceans and seas and I will do what it takes to let
you know that you can find hope in me.

Talk to me about it; lay your head on my breast.
Cry if you want to cry;
it makes you more of a man, not less.
This world can be treacherous
for a man that's trying to make it.
What I am offering is real.
You won't ever catch me trying to fake it.
When this world blows thru you like a cold January wind
knock on my heart, knock on my understanding,
knock on my love for you and I will let you in.

A man like you has many battles to fight.
Sometimes he needs someone there morning, noon or night.
When everything around you is crumbling,
when your life is in turmoil and your confidence is tumbling, just
make it to me or call me on the phone.
We can work out anything that's wrong.

I am in your corner whether you are up or down.
I am always close by; all you have to do is turn around.

Tonight We Make Love
With Our Clothes On

Imagine that we taste each other's kisses like sweet wine and get
carried away by the nectar that is yours and mine.
Explore my body, stopping to take in my womanhood as we make
love with our clothes on.

I imagine you beside me in the splendor of your nakedness.
I enjoy this imagination but I appreciate your willingness
to wait until the time is right.
So we make love with our eyes, our touch, with our clothes on tonight.

Our souls interlock as we become one in a special way.
I touch you but only with my mind today.
We hold hands tightly and cling to this wonder of love.
Love patient, love strong and love worth waiting for.
We both agree that we will wait a little longer
before we walk through ecstasy's open door.

You enter my mind with your questions and my answers
let you roam slowly through my past and present.
We try to learn each other's desires and secrets and we try to see if
we fit neatly into each other's future plans.

We know that our bodies desire to touch but we need to know if our
minds need each other as much.
Tonight we make love with our clothes on.
We talk, we laugh and we wink playfully.

We listen to the fireplace and watch the sparks
but we don't give in to passion tonight in the dark.

Your silk shirt never leaves your body but I do admire
the way that it clings to your chest and my flattering dress never gets
unbuttoned but it does cling tightly to my breast.
I feel the rumble in your soul and I can tell you feel it too.
It's the rumble from two hearts connecting in a way that's true.

The Composer of My Love

Your melody, your serenade, the keys of my heart
on which they are played.
Your melancholy lullaby, so sweet from you to me
that it makes me cry.
This enchanted moment, can I freeze it in time?
Promise me that every key that you play will be only mine?
A composer extraordinaire that is surely what you are.

You compose my heart's happiness so complete that the melodies
float off among the stars.
A symphony conductor so in tuned to my heart's orchestra. No
instrument is out of tune as long as you control my heart's chords.

You are a master musician playing soft on a golden harp and in each
chord you promise that we will never part.
The composer of my love?
From every corner of this earth your heart's music plays only for me
and it's so clear for me to hear.
It's as though the sound of your love for me vibrates
from the beauty of Paris to the Cathedrals of Rome.
So beautiful a love song not even the greatest composer
has ever known.

My love plays to royalty because to me that's what you are.
My love sends a melody on dove's wings but never too far.
I get the message that you send in the melody of each song.
I hear in each drum beat the magnitude of your love.
I hear in each piano key just how much this love means.
I hear in each blow of the saxophone the promise that you make to
always come home.

My love, my composer of my heart's greatest joy.

My love, my musical genius who serenades me near or far.

My love, my composer of the love that flows from me.

No matter how far you go I will always be in your love's audience for you to see.

Close Your Eyes and Come With Me

Close your eyes and come with me.
Let yourself go baby, let your mind, body and soul run free.
Give up your inhibitions and walk slowly into my arms.
I am trying to love you baby, not trying to do you harm.

Close your eyes and come with me.
I will guide you,
I will be your eyes,
I will light the path to your deepest and strongest desires.
Everything that you have held back let it go, let it flow.
I am going to water it like a flower and
together we will watch love grow.

Close your eyes and let every negative feeling subside.
Take my hand and hold it tight.
Take my heart baby and not just for tonight.
Take my soul baby and let it connect with yours.
It's you that I adore.

Close your eyes and imagine us on an endless sea of love.
The last heartache that you had we won't even speak of.
Now open your eyes and see this for what it is.
Look at me and see the love that is for you here.

A Remedy For Two Lonely Hearts

When the loneliness starts to cut you deep,
when you toss and turn but can't get to sleep,
pick up the phone and call me.
The day is done and I am at home.
Late in the evenings I have nothing to do.
I am here waiting for the loneliness to get to you.

When the loneliness starts to tear you up inside and
there is no place you can take your heart and hide
pick up your phone.
The day is done and I am waiting at home.
I get kind of lonely and I know that you do too.
You can comfort me and I can comfort you.

When the loneliness has you pacing the floor,
when you have tried to fulfill the emptiness
but nothing works anymore.
Pick up the phone.
I am waiting at home.
It's a place to start and a remedy for two lonesome hearts.

Some company and some conversation,
don't you think that would be nice?
If you stop me as I am leaving I just
might stay with you thru the night.
It's a place to start and a remedy for two lonesome hearts.

Let Me Stay Here For A While

Let me stay here for a while.
I will wipe your tears and make you smile.
Won't you please get to know me?
I am sure that I can make you happy.
You may find that you want me here all the time.
You can hold onto that hurt forever or you
can let go of the past hurt and let's get together.

Let me stay here for a while.
I will bring back your laughter and rekindle your joy.
You just might like having me around and
that's all right because I am ready to settle down.
Let me stay here for a while.
What are you afraid of?
Haven't you ever been offered true love?

I will hold you through your lonely moments and put
peace in your restless nights and when past memories
make you cry softly I will hold you until the daylight.
I believe that you will ask me to stay always.
Let me be there at the end of your good and bad days.

Let me stay here for a while.
You just might want me to stay with you
throughout eternity.
Let me stay here for a while and teach you to trust again.
Let me stay here for a while, first as your friend!

What Do I Want, What Will I Give

What Do I Want?

I want you to come home to me when the day is done.

I want you to think about me when I am not in your arms.

I want you to love me enough to work out the problems
that occur.
You can look at another woman but don't leave me
for her.

I want you to need me twenty-four hours a day and I will
do all I can to make sure that you always feel this
way.

I want you to hold me when my world spins out of control.
Take me away somewhere that only lovers go.

I want you to walk with me in love not yet explored.
Take my hand, hold it tight and know that I am
always yours.

I want you to smile when I cross your mind,
and if we disagree, and we will disagree,
there is a balance that people in love must find.

I want your soul, but not so that I can take control.

I want your heart, all the way to the deepest part.

I want all you have to give for as long as you live.

What Will I Give?

I will give you all of me.

I will give you quiet nights and calm memories.

I will give you peace in the middle of your desperation.

I will give you love without hesitation.

I will work out the bad times with you if it takes all night.
I know that we must work at love to get it right.

I will hold you without choking you.

I will love you without taking away your identity.
When we are apart, I will keep you in my heart.

I will give you silence when you need quiet.
I will give you space when you need to be alone.
I will give you solitude and a heart that does not roam.
I will give you all of the lovemaking you can take.
I will give you heated nights of passion and touches that cause a chain reaction.

I will share the gentle breezes of summer nights and
I will warm your winters like a candlelight.

I will give you smiles for no reason.

I will give you warmth in the coldest of seasons.

I will be your lover but more than that,

I will be your friend.

Your Love Calms Me

I was the storm and you were the calm.
You could settle me down when I am in your arms.
I was the hurricane and you were the quiet sea.
You could calm every volcano that erupted inside of me.
I was the thunder and the lightning and you were
the soft falling rain of a summer day.
Your sprinkles washed all of the thunder
inside of me away.

I was the uneasy one and you were the calm.
I was the uncertain tomorrow.
You were the bankable future.
I was the anguish and torment of past love lost.
You were the loving heart that made me forget it all.
I was the tornado, fierce winds of a broken soul.
You were the gentle summer breeze
that blew my way and made me whole.

Now I am quiet with you.
The seashores of my life are calm too.
Now I am a warm summer night
in tune with your gentle falling rain.

Now I am a soothing melody
in tune with your soft refrain.
With you I am calm.

I learned this in your arms.
I thought that mine was an incurable
broken heart but you are the cure.
Your love calms me.

Private Holiday

Can we get away,
take a private holiday and not do anything?
Let's relive our young dreams?
I feel like we're losing touch; I don't want to lose this love.
Can we pack a few things in a bag and drive out of town?
Find a lover's hideaway and just sit back and settle down?

Can we get away,
take a private holiday and not do anything?
We won't tell anyone where we're going
or when we'll be back.
Can we get away, how would you like that?
I want to walk on the beach with you and watch
the moon in your eyes and watch the sun set too.

Can we get away,
take a private holiday and not do anything?
Day-to-day routines, keeping up with our dreams
and that's okay.
Honey I think it's time that we took a break and got away.
I don't think that this love is in danger.
I just don't want to wake up one day and find
myself sleeping with a stranger.
I want to take you away from here and
get to know you all over again my dear.
Can we get away, take a private holiday?

Let Me Teach You

Let me teach you about tenderness.
I can tell you have had a cold life.
Somebody did you wrong.
I can do you so right.
Let me teach you about love that is forever.
It's a lesson that is so easy to learn.

Let me teach you how to open your mind.
Let me teach you how to open your heart.
Give your love to me.
We can tear the old hurt apart.
It's a slow journey to learning how to trust again.
I am willing to teach you if you open up and let me in.

I can tell you have had a cold life.
Somebody did you wrong.
I can do you so right.
Let me teach you.

It's All right

How easily you break me down.
You play my heartstrings like they were a violin.
I give in to you again and again.
It must be magic how you entice me.
You must have a spell on me that I can't see.
I am not complaining, not a bit.
Keep on doing what you are doing.
It's all right, I like it.

You keep me in a trance.
My eyes only see you.
It's all right because I affect
you the same way too.
If you have got me bewitched,
if you have cast a spell,
then I am yours for the rest of my life.

In The Quiet of The Evening

In the quiet of the evening, sun is setting, day is done.
We lay here in each other's arms.
This time together means so much.
We get lost in each other's touch.
Our desires run high.
We need each other so bad we could cry.
We forget about the problems of the day.
Lost in this bliss, wrapped up in this kiss.

In the quiet of the evening,
I slip into something comfortable.
You watch me with your eyes so full of love.
There are no sounds but yours and mine.
It's the moans from the ecstasy from
the gentle way you touch me.
I don't ever want to leave this quiet of the evening.
Telephone might ring, but it doesn't mean a thing.
We put on the answering machine.
Each evening is a new beginning.
In the quiet of the evening
I know our love is winning.

In the quiet of the evening,
sun is setting, day is done.
We lay here in each other's arms.
This time we spend together means so much.
We get lost in each other's touch.
We need each other so bad we could cry.
Forget about the problems of the day.
I always want to spend my evenings this way.

Friends and Lovers

Friends and lovers, lovers and friends.
Relationships that start out like this
go on and on with no end.
Before I was your lover, I was your friend.
I took the time to get to know you
and find out what you were going through
and I slowly, slowly learned to love you.

Friends and lovers, lovers and friends.
If I see you looking sad, I want to know why.
Never going to let this love die.
I am so close to you.
I know your every heartbeat.
It beats in time with mine.
If something troubles you,
it troubles me too.
We learned to care for each other
before we became lovers.

Friends and lovers, lovers and friends.
Quiet conversations like friends
or making love all night, again and again.
So much respect I have for you.
Friends and lovers, lovers and friends.

We built this foundation on a friendship so strong.
When we disagree, we never let it destroy you and me.
First of all, we were friends.
    I always want you in my life.
    From a friendship I became your wife.
Friends and lovers, lovers and friends.

In My Heart, In My Soul, In My Lifetime

In My Heart,   I believe in you.
In My Heart,   I put my trust in you.
In My Heart,   I know that you can make my dreams come true.

In My Soul,   You are my reason for going on.
In My Soul,   I know that I have found that pot of gold.
In My Soul,   I know that I exist only for you.

In My Lifetime, I will love no one but you.
In My Lifetime, I will know true love only through you.
                 At the end of my lifetime,
                 I will stop and thank you for loving me.
                 With the last breath in my body
                 I will say, "I Love You".

I Will

I will let you run to me
when you can't take anymore.
That is what I will be here for.

I will let you hide out
and rest comfortably
here with me.

I will let you run to me
when you can't go another step further.
I will always be here,
you won't ever need another.

I will talk, if you want to talk.
If you want some peace,
we can just sit quietly.
What I am trying to say is,
I will fulfill all of your needs.
I will be everything a woman can be.

Here and Now

Here and Now, we are all there is.
Close the world outside.
Turn the key in the lock.
Kiss me and never stop.
Imagine that we are on an island
and there is no one but you and me.
We are all there will ever be.

Here and Now, we are all there is.
In the tenderness of your caresses,
I could get lost and never return.
For the touch of your hands, my body burns.
Lay here with me on into the dawn.
You and I are all there is.
Everybody else is gone.

Here and Now, we are all there is.
You are my past, my future and my destiny.
All the things I need, you give to me.
Smile at me and thrill me.
You have the power to do that.
Here and Now, we are all there is.

Take It Slow

I am the kind of woman who likes to take it slow.
Examine my options and decide which way to go.
So when you move on me, don't move too fast because I will not
think that you are sincere and this will not last.

I want to get to know your soul and mind and
I can only do that if we spend some time.
When you move on me don't move too quick.
I won't think that you are sincere and I will not accept it.
I ease into things kind of laid back and slow.
I examine my options and decide which way to go.

Don't impress me with material things.
I have been offered more of them than
the average woman has seen.
But if you spend some time that stays on my mind.
Don't buy me furs.
I have turned them down already.
I just like it when you come to me slow and steady.

Rainy Day

It's a rainy day but it doesn't matter much.
This is the kind of weather
when everybody runs for shelter.
Laying here in each other's arms.
The rain falling outside can't do us any harm.

It's a rainy day, but we don't mind.
It can rain until the end of the time.
Outside the window
people are running to and fro,
trying to hurry up and
get to where they have to go.

It's a rainy day.
I took off from work today
and so did you.
We will just lay here until
the rain is through.
On our window raindrops splatter.
but this love we are making inside
it does not get any better.

Winter and Your Love

The leaves are falling from the trees
and gathering gold and orange on the ground.
The wind blew so hard it twisted my dress around.
A chill was in the air but your warm love was there
so I didn't really care.

The last days of summer were upon us.
I knew that soon winter would settle in.
I also knew that the warmth of your love would
warm me again and again.

A cold rain fell last night and with it came a late night freeze. In our
room it was blazing hot because your body lay next to me. As we
awoke the weatherman said heavy snow was sure to fall.
I was warm inside because you said sometime today
you would stop and give me a call.

Winter comes in like a lion, so strong and chilling.
I am kept so warm inside by your love that is so fulfilling.
We roast marshmallows by the fireplace.
We stand in the window together and watch as winter covers
everything with a haze.

Hot apple cider or sipping warm cocoa.
Laying here in your arms I don't care
how hard the wind blows.
No cold wind can get through your hot, hot kiss.
No winter storm can match your smoldering hot touch.
Against anything winter brings with it you warm me so much.

How You Love Me

You notice when I get my hair cut and
when I buy a new dress.
You take time to say that you love me
and I don't have to guess.
You hold me like we just met every time you hold me.
You let me be me, oh, how you love me!

If someone makes me cry, you kiss away my tears.
But you never make me cry.
You take my frown and turn it upside down
and you paint all my days with a smile.
How you love me just drives me wild.

You hold my hand when we walk.
You even listen when I talk.
You make me feel like our love is real.
How you love me!

All man, you really are.
That's why you are man enough to show
how you love me!

I am careful with the love you give.
I don't take it for granted.
I appreciate the love you give.
Thanks for the seeds of love you have planted.

How you love me sends me spinning like a child in a schoolyard.
How you love me makes loving you easy, not hard.
How you love me!

It's Love

It's a ruthless game, give it a ruthless name but it's love.
It's a damned if you do, damned if you don't.
Give it any kind of name that you want but it's love.
Call it sentimental, call it dangerous and gentle, it's love.
It's something that your daddy did and your mother did too. You
don't get out of this world without it happening to you.
Curse it all night and say it isn't right but it's love.
It's like cocaine but it takes over the heart before it takes over the
brain.
You can't take a hit and quit because it pulls you in too deep, it's love.

Your sister fell into it, you said that you don't understand but it's love.
Keep on living, baby, it's coming for you, it's love.
Kings give up thrones for it.
Emperors give up the right to rule.
If it got to them it will get to you, it's love.
When it's love it's not like wham bam, thank you mam!
It can bring a strong man to his knees.
It can make a woman "beg" take me back please.

Man nor woman can't really explain it.
Call it anything that you want to but it's love no matter what you
name it.
It makes sons tell their moms treat her right because she is the one.
It makes daughters tell their daddies step back and don't interfere
because I am in love and I need him here.

Call it voodoo; call it anything that you want to, it's love.

It has been here since the beginning of time.

It made Adam eat the apple and I think he knew that Eve was lying, but it was love.

It's a ruthless game; call it a ruthless name but it's love.

Call it anything that you want to but it will get to you.

Chapter 2
LOVE LOST

People Take

They take your soul if you let them
and leave you hollow inside.
They take your smile and in its place
they leave you with a frown.
PEOPLE TAKE,
because they have not learned how to
GIVE AND TAKE!

They take your kindness and compassion and
and leave you afraid to love again.
They take your invitation of come on in
and before you know it they are gone again,
and how lonely you stand there.
They take your dreams and shatter them,
leaving you only nightmares.
PEOPLE TAKE,
because they have not learned how to
GIVE AND TAKE!

They take nights of passion from you
and in the morning they don't care.
Offer them your breast to lay their head for a time.
They rest comfortably and laugh at you in their mind.
PEOPLE TAKE,
because they have not learned how to
GIVE AND TAKE!

Cry A Little For Me

Cry a little for me.

I have cried rivers for you.

You should cry for me too.
Sing the blues a little over me.
Lord knows I have sung it enough over you.
Feel some of the pain I have felt.
Go through the changes I have gone through.

Moan a little for me.
Call my name in vain,
like I have called yours.
Pace the floor at night,
like I have paced for you.

Wonder where the hell I am,
like I have wondered too.

Cry a little for me.

I have cried rivers for you.

We Tried

We gave it all we could.

But it didn't do any good.
I guess it wasn't meant to be.
This love between you and me.
What are the tears for?
We tried!

What are the memories of the years for?
We will keep them locked up inside and
someday when the pain becomes too much to bare,
we will recall memories buried deep somewhere.

I hope the past isn't all we live for.

I hope we find other lovers once more.

We tried!

I Had

I had that pot of gold at the end of the rainbow.
I had that four leaf clover that
people search for over and over.
I touched that untouchable something and I
came to know the true meaning of love.
Love blossomed like a flower and all too soon it died.

I had my arms around a love
that was, oh so, hard to hold.
I loosened my grip for a moment
or did I just let it go?
When I reached for it again,
it was, oh so, cold.

I Am

I am the moment in time that you froze because it was easier than loving me.

I am the heartbeat that you skipped because you could not believe that your heart beat in time with mine.

I am the duet that you sang off key because you and I together were too sweet of a melody.

I am the wilted rose, because the red was too bright so you did not give our love water and you did not give it light.

I am the commitment that you never made.

Now you cry because if you had committed I would have stayed.

I am the longing that you never fulfilled.

I am the love you lost and you try to replace
but you never will.

I am the sunshine that you replaced with the torrid downpour of a storm.

I will always be here somewhere on your heart's distant horizon and you will always look for me because I will always be that once in a lifetime love that you lost.

I have moved on like the tumbleweed
travels against the wind.

I have moved on like the tide rolls out,
but unlike the tide, I will not roll in again.

I am the pillow you cling to because
my sweet aroma lingers there.

I am the sweet whispers that you dream at night
that I still give you in your ear.

Now I give my sweet whispers to someone else dear.

I am and always will be that love that you
can only touch in your memory.
You and I both know,
that I am the one who tried to love you.

The depth of my love you did not believe.

So I had to leave.

So Damn Stubborn

A silence you could cut with a knife.
A pain so deep the scars will never be erased.
A melody so sad that no one bothers to play it.
An apology is due and neither one of us will say it.

Years of planning destroyed with one night of
senseless arguments.
You will go your way and I will go mine.
So Damn Stubborn.

So easy, so easy to say, I am sorry.
The words will never be spoken.
The silence will never be broken.

I screamed, you screamed.
One heated night has destroyed so many dreams.
So Damn Stubborn.

I want to pull the words from your throat.
Please say that you are sorry.
You look at me longingly, deep into my eyes.
In your heart I hear you say, honey I apologize.

The words will never be spoken.

The silence will never be broken.

So stubborn, so stubborn, so damn stubborn.

I Walk Away

I compared you to the morning sunlight.
Then your light went dim.
I treasured you like a pot of gold.
If there are any gold pieces left I can't find them.

I longed for you like a junkie needing a fix.
Only to find out that maybe I don't need this.
I loved you better than I loved myself.
That was my first mistake so how dare
I to blame you for my heartache.

I gave up me to have you.
I breathed when you breathed.
I walked behind you, too far behind you.
Never side by side.
I gave up my dignity and then you took my pride.
I watched it happen, but worse, I let it happen.
I thought this was how love was supposed to be.
You commanded, I obeyed.
You threatened to go, I begged you to stay.
I thought I was loving you, showing that I could be true.

I stepped out of the haze today.
The sun shined through and the clouds rolled away.
I took a look at you and I didn't know you.
I took a look at you and I didn't love you.
But worst of all, I took a look at me.
and I cried for what I had become.

How did I loose me? When did I loose me?
You watch me with disbelief as I cry and pack to leave.
You stand in awe and say that I will never truly walk away.
I put my suitcase down. I wipe my tears and I stand erect, which is
hard to do after bending for so many years.

I leave the material things.
I leave the house and I leave your dreams.
I leave you standing there like a fool.
I walk away with the only thing that is real and true.
I walk away with my pride intact.
I walk away with my soul restored.
I walk away with my sanity slowly returning.
I walk away with me, the me that use to be.

Love Lost Too Fast

Like sand in a hour glass,
You slipped through my heart too fast.

Like time in motion that never stops.
I tried to hold on to you.
But memories are all I have got.
Like the cry of a child that travels off in space.
I wanted so badly to always look upon your face.

How did I let you get away?
Did I do all I could to make you stay?

Now I sit here looking at pictures,
the past of you and me.
Now I wonder why, how and when
did it all come unglued.
Like sand in an hour glass,
you slipped through my heart too fast.

I wanted to hold you always and forever.
But now I think I will see you again, never.

You Are

You are a memory buried, but not forgotten.
You are love lost, but often thought of.
You are the coolness of the wind, blowing gently on my face.
You are the echoes of the past that occupy my space.
You are the sunrise that bathes me in its glory.
You are the first chapter in my life if anyone ever tells
      my story.

You are a memory buried, but not forgotten.
You are the waves that splash pleasantly along the seashore but
      your love washed out of my life,
      never to return anymore.
You are the moon overhead that breaks the darkness
      with a little bit of light.
You are the whistle in my teapot that tells me the water
      for my tea is ready.
You are the shadow in my cup that reminds me that I have
      loved and lost someone.

You are a memory buried, but not forgotten.
You are the calm of a spring day.
You are autumn in all its beauty that takes my breath away
You are a memory buried, but not forgotten.

Where Did It Go

What happened to the laughter?
It was replaced by tears.
What happened to the tenderness?
It disappeared with the years.
I want it back the way it was.
I am fighting to hold on to your love.
Where did it go?

That distant look in your eyes,
where did it come from?
I use to see only love in your eyes
when you take me in your arms.
Your touches are now so cold.
I just want to know,
where did it go?

A Distant Heartbeat

A distant heartbeat in a distant time.
A memory that boggles the mind.
A love that did not last.
A cry from the past.

A promise made and broken.
Things he forgot to take left behind as tokens.
A melody once played on ivory keys,
now so sad it makes me fall to my knees.

A stranger in the street who looked like you.
I rushed after him but the face was not true.
A wedding ring in a jewelry box,
whose sparkle lasted longer than ours.
A ribbon I still have from my bridal shower.

A bed we picked out together that I now sleep in alone.
A room where I wake up screaming from the pain of having you gone.
A chance to hold and have love, but we blew it.
A love we should have fought to keep, but we didn't do it.

Now two souls tormented.
Two hearts searching for love again.
Will we ever find someone to shield us
from lost love's fierce winds?

Who Will Apologize

Silence in the night that neither one of us will break.
Steps toward each other that neither one of us will take.
In stubborn and unbroken silence we slowly let love die.
So determined not to give in, you nor I.

You won't say it and I don't dare.
In separate beds we lose a little
more of our love somewhere.
Days of silence turned into weeks.
Weeks without touching turned into months.

Finally the silence was broken for one of us to say,
better we should separate than live this way.

In our eyes we ask, who will apologize.

We divided everything and started life alone again.
Here I am missing you and there you are missing me.
Neither one of us remembering why we disagreed.

This Love Is Running Out Of time

This love is running out of time.
It's slowly, slowly dying.
We are losing ground so fast.
Clinging so tight to the past.
It's hard, but we must admit.
Neither one of us are trying to save it.
Losing a little more love every day.

This love is running out of time.
It's just a matter of days.
Soon we will go our separate ways.
I know and you do too
but neither one of us cares.
We will just hold on until
there is only hatred here.

This love is running out of time.
Like watching sand in an hourglass.
This love is fading so fast.
Like a prisoner on death row,
one day we will have to go.
We have moved into separate rooms
and we don't talk anymore.

When Hearts Collide

When hearts collide like two trains on a track there
isn't much you can do to repair heartbreak like that.
When hearts grow cold that once were warm.
When pain is all there is, in what once were loving arms.
There is nothing you can do but accept it and move on.

When the touch of each other makes you long for more
it's time for one of you to walk out of the door.
When he dreams of a lady like the one who lives next door
it's time to admit that we don't have what we had before.
When the past has good memories but there are none now,
it's time to admit that love died somewhere, somehow.

When she longs for him to stay gone forever and a day.
When he never notices if she is gone away.
It's time to admit that we can't live this scene in life's play.
When your looks at each other are as cold as steel.
No one admits anymore how they really feel.
It's time to part and let the heartbreak start to heal.

Be man enough to say so long.
Be woman enough to say it was good when it was good.
Be man enough to say we both know that it's gone.
Be man and woman enough to hope you find love again.
When hearts collide you should walk away while the two
of you can still be past lovers and future friends.

Today, Tonight, I Thought of You

Today   I thought of you and my body ached.
Today   I thought of you and I knew my soul would break.
Today   I thought of you like memories on a cloud.
Today   I thought of you and wanted to scream out loud.

Today   I thought of you and fell to my knees from the pain
of losing you.
Today   I thought of you and the mind blowing things we
use to do.
Today   I thought of you and my eyes filled with tears.
Today   I thought of you and longed for the gone years.

Today   I thought of you and my world split apart.
Today   I thought of you and I grabbed my chest for fear
of dropping my heart.
Today   I thought of you and the day grew dark and dreary.
Today   I thought of your eyes that were once so
captivating.

Tonight I laid in bed alone and inhaled the scent of you that lingered
behind even though you were long gone.
Tonight I tossed and turned in the pain of lost ecstasy.
Tonight I climbed the walls remembering what you use to
do to me.
Tonight I held a pillow in my hands that use to hold a man.
Tonight I dreamed of you touching every part of me,
holding me close and bringing me to my knees.

Tonight, I cursed your memory when I awoke and I was all
alone.
Tonight, I faced the reality that you are really, really gone.

The Pain of Losing You

I watched the snow fall down all white and untouched before it reached the ground.
I wondered why our love couldn't remain untouched.
Untouched by the lies, the nights of screams
and the heartaches that destroyed so many dreams.

I walked to the kitchen and put the water on for tea.
I wondered how we let this thing happen to you and me.
As the water boiled and the teakettle screamed,
I screamed also from somewhere deep inside my soul.
How did we let this pain take such control?

I poured my tea and watched the cup fill up.
I wondered why we couldn't stay full of our love.
I paced the floor and stopped to look out of the window.
The snow had stopped falling and you had stopped calling.
The pain cut me deeper than I could stand.
I dropped the cup and cried as it fell from my hand.
It broke into pieces and shattered just like you and I.
I couldn't sweep up the pieces no matter how hard I tried.

I walked the few steps back to my bed.
I pulled the covers over my head.
I tried to shield myself from the cold but it followed me under the covers and made me remember when we lovers.
I screamed for the ghosts to go away but they circled my heart and made a promise to always stay.

My pillow became wet with tears.
My heart became frozen with fears.
My soul screamed for the lost, lonely and empty years.

When loosing you hurt so bad that I could not breathe, sleep, welcomed sleep, came and took me.

My heart was quiet and my soul was calm.

I drifted off somewhere to days long gone.

I Use To Know

I use to know the scent of you.
Sweet like a summer morning dew.
But not anymore.

I use to know the touch of you.
Tender like a baby brand new.
But not anymore.

I use to know the kiss of you.
Soft against my skin like the brush
of a summer wind.
But not anymore.

I use to know that look in your eyes
that held me captive and kept me hypnotized.
Sweet words use to fall from your lips
just like honey drips.
But not anymore.

Ending Like This

I never wanted us to end like this.
I always thought I would share your tender kiss.
Never dreamed, in my worst nightmares, that
I would wake up and you would not be there.
We are packing our bags
and the house has been sold.
Never wanted us to end like this.
I will miss your kiss.

We couldn't settle things.
We couldn't hear each other
in between the screams.
I never wanted us to end like this.
Nothing but coldness in our eyes
and storm in our touch.
I hate ending like this so very much.

Somewhere In The Middle

Somewhere in the middle of the madness.
Somewhere in the middle of the pain,
I looked up and saw you coming again.

Somewhere in the middle of the madness,
somewhere in the middle of pain,
I remembered when you walked out
and left me crying like falling rain.
How dare you come around here again?

Somewhere in the middle of the healing
you stirred up old feelings.
Somewhere in the middle of getting over you
I looked up and saw you coming again.
I swiped away a tear for a moment or two.
Just long enough to remember the
hell you put me through.
I cleared my head for a second or so and
remembered when I begged you not to go.
What happened, did your new love finally grow old?
You reached out to touch me and my body went cold.

Somewhere in the middle of the nights alone
you apologized for doing me wrong.
Somewhere in the middle of getting over you,
you came back and tried to explain
the hell you put me through.

Somewhere in the middle of you asking can we try again?
I realized that you did me a favor when you made our love end; so I
stopped you in the middle of you begging me to take you back;
I looked at you and I said, sorry, but I just can't do that.

It's Over

It's over, the curtains blowing in the breeze know it.
It's over, the look of longing on your face shows it.
It's over; the missing late night interludes whisper it in the night.
It's over, gone away like the dove that takes flight.

It's over, our friends can tell because we don't do anything together
anymore.
It's over, you don't respond to my touches like before.
It isn't just over for you. It's over for me too.
It's over, I have no desire to make love to you and it's
clear to see that you have lost the desire for me.

It's over, We do not argue nor do we blame each other.
We're both mature enough to know
that people often just stop loving.
It's over, I can hear the message being carried on the
wind never to be reborn again.
It's over, and now and then I feel like I should cry.
It's over, the tears won't fall and I know the reason why.
I know that it does not mean that you hate me
and it does not mean that I hate you.
It simply means that it's over.
It simply means that our love is through.

Chapter 2

LOVE LONGED FOR

Desperate Times

These are desperate times we live in
when it's love we are trying to save.
The desperation overwhelms us
when it seems that love is slipping away.

I dread the thought of starting over with
someone new; someone who is not you.
I have become accustomed to your touch
and the aroma of your smell.
I don't want to learn these things
from someone else.

The desperation rises and threatens to
choke the life from me.
I am fighting to hold on to you and
at the same time keep my sanity.
What is it that you need that you
can't get from me?

Is it the color of my hair?
I can change it to a different shade.
Is it the scent of my cologne?
I can throw that bottle away.
Is it the same face in the morning that you see?
I can do so many things so that I won't look like me.

These are desperate times we live in
when it's love we are trying to save.

Fleeting Moments

A chance for happiness.
A second so short it seems we never really lived it all.
A taste of bliss and joy.
A yearning for what we had and let slip away;
like sand that slips through our hands.
Fleeting moments.

A second of love that we stole.
I wanted so badly to keep you here.
I watched as you walked away.
I dared not run after you.
I knew you had to go.
Fleeting moments.

I stood there and tears stained my face.
For a moment, my soul left my body
and I begged you not to go.
I feel as though my life is truly through.
For so fleeting a moment,
I have loved and lost you.

Something Unspoken Here

There is something unspoken here.
Vows taken but broken here.
I think we should talk.
I don't want to pack and walk.
There is a love I am trying to save here.
I think we should talk, my dear.

There is a desire that burns hotter than any fire
and it needs to be fulfilled.
There is something unspoken here.
I think we should talk my dear.

There is a look in your eyes here
and I'm afraid you are drifting away.

There is a strong need in me to beg you to stay.
There is something unspoken here.
Vows taken but broken here.
I think we should talk my dear.

In A Maze Called Life

In a maze called life, I wonder aimlessly
trying to find the exit that leads to eternal peace
but every turn leads to heartache and sorrow.
Will I find the exit to love tomorrow?

In a maze called life, I take another wrong turn,
and try to chalk it up as another lesson learned.
In a maze called life, I stumble blindly, reaching for
and needing something that I can't seem to find at any exit.
In a maze called life, I get caught up in the need
for more, but more of what?
I get stranded in my thoughts and lost in my wishes.

In a maze called life, I search for forever friendship
and unending passionate kisses.

In a maze called life,
I twist, I turn and I go in and out
of unnecessary avenues.

Hoping, longing, praying that one twist, one turn will lead me to
someone true.

I Keep Searching

I keep searching for that unobtainable thing,
that love everlasting that I find in my dreams.
That kind of partnership that says I'm for you and you're for me and
we fulfill each other needs.
I keep searching for that wondrous kind of love
that seems to slip through so many fingers.
Years pass and something dies and the
love we had never ever lingers.

I keep searching for one person who realizes that
to share this common bond is what we were put here for.
I keep searching for someone who understands
that I am all they will ever need and with me
they will need nothing more.
Someone to share the ups, the downs, the smiles, the tears,
the triumps as well as the defeats.
Someone who will enjoy the summer breezes
and weather winter's storms with me.

I keep searching for someone true who
won't stray away from me for someone new.
I keep searching for someone who will tell me
what they want so that I can give them all they desire.
Someone who will warn me if I'm ever in danger
of putting out our love's fire.
Someone who will talk to me and share their life's adventures and
someone who will look into my eyes,
deep into my eyes, and find the gleam they put there.
Someone who will be honest, true and hold steadfast.
I keep searching for someone to love and someone
to take my love and treat it always as if it is new.
I keep searching and I will search until I die.
If I don't find this true love it won't be because I didn't try.

Who Do We Blame

After all is said and done, who do we blame?
No more words to be spoken, what do we do?
Time is so short it seems and so quickly we
loose our dreams.
The laughter is so quick to fade.
The pain lingers on for days.

After the smiles have stopped
and the tears start to flow
who do we blame, where do we go.
When everything we have together
turns into nothing but regret,
who do we blame?

After all the promises we made fall through
and there seems to be nothing more we can do,
who do we blame?
When the kind words are replaced
with only harsh ones,
how do we figure out what went wrong?
Who do we really put the blame on?

The Storm In My Heart

Yesterday was endless and my head was cloudy all day.
Last night was long and lingering and the time in between the day
and night was agonizing and filled with despair.
You danced in my head constant and always.
You played on my mind endlessly and
lingered forever in my memory.

A storm has been forecasted to settle in around midnight.
But not even the thundering and lightning
will be a match for this storm in my heart.
The weatherman is predicting torrential rains
but no rains can match my tears.

I sat in the dark and watched and listened
as the thunder roared like a lion.
But inside my soul roared even louder.
I watched as the lightning struck every corner of the house
and the pain struck every corner of my heart!

With each crack of thunder and every drop of rain.
I paced the floor in hopes of shutting out the pain.
I turned up the heat to warm myself from the
coldness the storm brought with it.
But that did nothing to warm the chill in my heart.

I hurried to bed and prayed for sleep to take me.
I longed to shut out the storm inside me
that blew its fierce winds against my soul
and circled me with its loud echoes of love lost
but never forgotten.

I closed my eyes and begged for sleep
and as the night wore on,
God in his mercy gave me relief!
I drifted off to memories of
passionate nights with you,
walks on the beach for two,
candlelight dinners and bubbly champagne.
For a moment, a brief period in time,
the storm in my heart subsided and
I rested warmly in the memories.

Suddenly the crack of thunder awoke my heart.
The patter of the raindrops alerted my soul.
These memories are all I have because you have
taken your love and left me lonely and cold.
The storm in my heart once again raged louder
than the storm brewing outside.
I jumped out of bed, paced the floor and cried and cried!

I cried with each crack of thunder!
I cried with each raindrop that fell.
The storm in my heart raged like the fires of hell!

Autumn Came As A Thief

I watched the first signs of autumn
and a chill went through me.
Somehow I knew it was not from the autumn wind.
Why would the fall of a leaf cause me grief?
There was something here I couldn't explain.
I noticed you as I noticed Autumn too.
You were changing with her.

When Autumn's winds got cold enough
to run the children in from play
you seemed to move even farther away.
I sat by the window and watched Autumn
turn the green grass brown.
I watched her shake the trees down.
It seemed as though she knew that with each
change she made there was a change in you.

I remember nights when I could not feel Autumn's wind,
because you were touching me skin to skin.
Now her winds chill me deep.
You lay awake on your side of the
bed and never touch me.
Were you changing in the summer and I didn't notice?
Did you stop loving me in the Spring
and I never recognized a thing?

No conversation, no hesitation,
for I know that you must go.
Autumn, if you were a lady of shape or form
I would fight you for him but your howling winds
that say, follow me, I am no match for them.
Damn Autumn, I hear your howling laughter!
Once again, you have come and taken my man with you.
Hurry Summer and come!

She Longs

She longs for that which was and never will be again.
She opened up her heart and let a stranger in.
She gave in to nights of pleasure and pain.
The pleasure of his touches and the pain
of not knowing if he will ever come again.

She lived for him and him alone,
never stopping to think this might be wrong.
She longs for that which was and never will be again.
She has heard the song before that Only Fools Rush In.
But when your heart gets involved you don't remember
that first you should be friends.

She would cry if the tears would fall.
But they are stuck inside of her soul.
Her heartache is so strong that it won't let the tears flow.
She longs for that which was and never will be again.
She took a chance on love and it was not hers to win.

He made no promises; he came with no guarantees.
He never said that he would be all that she needs.
She knows she ran in too fast.
She never read the warning signs.
He went straight for her heart and bypassed her mind.

Now she longs for that which was and never will be again.
Touches in the night like sparks from a fireplace.
That tender, oh so, tender way he gently held her face.
The things they did together that drove her to the point of the ecstasy
of tears.
In his arms she should have been afraid but there she had no fear.

Her heart would not let her mind talk so she heard no words warning
her to be careful of this love.
She gave in, she gave her all and then he gave her up.

She doesn't blame him.

She wishes that she could.

She was in too deep.

She was in this for keeps.

He wasn't looking for anything
that held the promise of eternity.
Now she longs for that which was and never will be again.

Captive In His Bed

She aches for the man that she can never have
because the risk would be too much.
She has a yearning that can never be fulfilled.
For she belongs to another sealed with a wedding band
and the man that she aches for is best friends with her husband.

Her husband has already told her that if she leaves
the children must stay and if he had to he would
take her to court and take them away.
So she pretends to still love him but he knows that she dreams of
someone else but he does not know who.

The man who really loves her is waiting in anticipation
for something that may never come.
He aches to wipe her tears, shoulder her fears and keep her safe in
his arms.
He aches to treat her like the queen that she is and to her he would
be so good.
But she will not love him at the risk of losing her motherhood.
For next to loving him her children are her greatest joy.
So she stays with her husband so that she can stay with her little
girl and boy.

The man she aches for and the man who aches for her,
they exist in separate worlds clouded with unfulfilled love.
The man who aches for her does what he always does
he holds her in his heart and he holds her in his head.
She sleeps with her face to the wall for she no longer can sleep face
to face with the man she is married to
who holds her captive in his bed.

To You

To you, I was just another face in the crowd.
To you, I was just another heart you had won.
I wanted to be so much more to you than
just another somebody you stepped on.

I longed to be so many things to you.
I longed to have you with me always.
To you, I was a nobody going nowhere
just another place to rest your head.
My bed was just another bed.

I wanted to be so much more to you.
To you, I would have given so much.
But you gave me no more
than a yearning for tomorrow.

Money Does Not Buy Everything

You offered me champagne.
I only wanted you and a simple glass of wine.
You offered me shopping sprees in Paris.
I just wanted more of your time.
You offered me a Black Diamond mink.
I only wanted you to come home to me.

You offered me a Rolex for my birthday.
You had it delivered to me because you had to go away.
The glitter from the Rolex bounced off of the wall.
I set in my Black Diamond mind and waited for you to call.
You asked me to meet you at a five star restaurant.
You sent a limousine to pick me up.
You were two hours late.
The waiter said he called and he wants you to wait.
You walked in with a string of pearls and
that was supposed to make everything okay.

When I was with you I fell asleep on satin sheets.
Flannel would have been fine if you had slept
more often with me.
Your Secretary called to ask me if I had gotten the roses. She said,
oh by the way, he asked me to let you know
that he had to leave town today.
He said that he will call you as soon as he closes the deal.
You called and the phone rang.
Ring number one; I washed all of the champagne glasses so they
would be clean when you came home.
Ring number two; I packed away the pictures of my shopping spree
in Rome.
Ring number three; I laid the Black Diamond Mink on the couch
all neatly spread out.

Ring number four; I put the Rolex on the crisp satin sheets because I won't need it anymore.
Ring number five; I called a cab, not a limo.
Ring number six; I picked up my suitcase and walked out of the door.

Then my cell phone started to ring.
Ring number one; the cab drove by many five star restaurants that you have taken me to.
Ring number two; I forgot to take off the pearls so I will mail them back to you.

Today I live a simple life and I love a simple man.
We spend time together and we walk hand in hand.
Now and then I run into you and you ask can we try again?
I read about you in fancy magazines and I smile
because I know that you know now
that money does not buy everything.

Listen To The Howling Wind

Listen to the howling wind, blowing out and blowing in,
How do I chill myself against the coldness of the night?
How do I fall asleep when something doesn't feel right?
You should have been home a long time ago.
What will your excuse be this time, honey, I don't know.

Listen to the howling wind, blowing out and blowing in.
Why can't I make myself see the truth before my eyes?
Why can't I quit living in this fairytale and
stop believing in your lies?
I would fall asleep if I could and
dream about when this love was good.
I can't stop thinking.
I can't stop crying.
I can't believe this love is dying.

Listen to the howling wind, blowing out and blowing in.
I am not ready to give you up so I pretend not to know
what the wind howls against the door.
The message in the wind is clear.
You must be somewhere because you sure
as hell aren't here.

The Car Accident

She remembers his laughter.
She hears it echo off of every wall in the house.
She has packed his things now.
His cologne bottles are all gone
but their scent lingers on.
She finally gave his suits away today.
She knows that he would never wear them again.

It was a rainy night on a dark road and he was driving in.
The car went over the cliff and her heart went with it.
She wonders why they didn't pull her heart up with the wreckage.
Didn't they see it lying there?
Her soul had to be scattered around that accident somewhere.

They came by and rung the bell.
They told her what had happened and their words
condemned her heart to eternal hell.
She screamed, he's not dead.
He wouldn't leave me like that.

Without him I can't move on from where I am at.
They held her and tried to comfort her.
They told her she shouldn't view the body tonight.
She replied, I must see him because you just can't be right.

She knew it had to be somebody else.
Maybe somebody stole his car.
She could replace that but she couldn't replace her heart.

When they pulled the cover back from his face
the room she was standing in orbited into space.
She fell to the floor like a baby crying in pain.
She cried, he's not dead!

Somebody wake him up!
She knew that if loving him could bring him back then her love was
enough and he had loved her the same way.

Now she's finally giving up his things,
but she still wears the wedding ring.
One day she might take a ride to the spot where his car went down.
She might find her heart and soul there if she takes a look around.

I Am Feeling

I am feeling like I want to be held.
I am out here in this world all by myself
I am feeling like I want to be touched.
I need somebody's arms around me so much.
I am feeling like I got a need, a need
to have somebody right here with me.

I am feeling like my soul wants to cry.
This feeling of loneliness damn near makes me want to die.
One man, one man to fulfill all my aches and pains.
Take them away once and then take them away again.
It must be love I'm looking for.
Why won't it knock on my door?
I read about it in books.
I see it in movies.
They write it about in magazines.
I need it so bad I could scream.

I am feeling like I want to be held.
I am out here in this world all by myself.
I am feeling like I want to be touched.
I need somebody's arms around me so much.
I am feeling like I got a need, a need
to have somebody right here with me.

Saw a couple walking hand in hand.
I stopped and wondered where is my man?

The Passing Time

The seconds became minutes
and I never heard from you.
But I waited, just as I promised to do.

The minutes turned into hours.
I stood by the window,
thought about you and
cried with the April showers

The hours turned into days
and the tears stained my face.

The days became weeks.
To ask if I had a letter was the only
time I would speak.

The weeks grew into months
and I waited some more.

The months changed into years
and I shed more tears.

I Dream of A Love

I dream of a love that holds but does not bind.
I dream of a love the soft, strong, tender and sweet kind.
I dream of a love that calms my nights and soothes my
days.
I dream of a love that rocks me like a baby and takes my
worries away.
I dream of a love that covers me like satin sheets.
I dream of a love that wraps me up in arms manly but
tenderly.
I dream of a love that runs the distance and never quits.
I dream of a love that lets me rest in it and reassures me
that this is total bliss.

I dream of a love that surrounds me like the Heavens
surround the stars.
I dream of a love that protects my heart.
I dream of a love Tantalizing, mesmerizing.
I dream of a love with such fierce desire that nothing can
match the need.

I dream of a love that makes me happy and never brings
me fear.
I dream of a love at night that boils such passion in me
that I give in, give up and cry from the
touch of you.
I dream of a love that takes me places that I never knew.
I dream of a love like this, your touch and your kiss.
I long to find this kind of love and not just dream of it.
I could cry out, I could scream for my soul dreams
and dreams of a love like this.
It's not rain that is pain, splashing against my soul.
For I dream of a love in desperation that I can always have and hold.

What Happened To Us

All the laughter, all the good times
and all the joy we knew boy.
What happened to us?
We got caught up in this vicious circle of life.
If we let it, it will destroy a husband and a wife.
Instead of holding on through the roughest storms
we drifted away on the windy seas.
When we reached for each other again,
I couldn't find you and you couldn't find me.

What happened to us?
We swore we wouldn't fall into that trap.
We didn't know love was dying
until it was already dead.
I lost count of the nights that
we feel asleep in separate beds.

What happened to us?
We got caught up in life's whirlwind.
Is there a chance that we will ever love again?
I'm told that most lovers don't survive.
Now when we look at each other
there are so many questions in our eyes.
What happened to us?

I Thought We Had It All

Shadows dancing off the wall.

Memories too painful to recall.

I would have sworn that you and I had it all.
Now my tears mix with the raindrops
and this ache in my heart never stops.

I remember laughter but it faded too quick.
I recall wedding vows that said we would
stay together through thin and thick.
I thought we had it all.

Everyday finds me reminiscing and
sitting here missing your kissing.
Oh, how fast the promises were broken.
Now between us, no words of love are ever spoken.
I thought we had it all.

We were foolish enough to believe
that our love would beat the odds.
We thought we could survive the worst of times.
Now I stand here hungering for love
that once was yours and mine.
I thought we had it all.

How did we lose it? Why did we let it die?
I know I will spend days wondering why.
You won't talk about what went wrong with us
and when I try, I just break down and cry.

My heart knows that I will never love like this again.

When it's over, truly over, the pain is too much to bare.

I'm left here lingering on the edge somewhere.
Here I am with memories too painful,
much too painful to recall.

Shadows dancing off the wall.

Memories too painful to recall.

I was foolish enough to think that you and I had it all.

She

She cries at touching love scenes and she makes love to the love of her life in her deepest dreams.

She protects her heart with a coat of armor that is hard to break and she has earned every line of loneliness on her face.

She is gentle but not many people know that because she hides her gentleness well.
She is determined not to let anyone put her heart thru hell.

She longs for a love that will withstand the test of time.
A love that calms the longing in her heart and eases her restless mind.

She is a contrast of personalities.
She is a patchwork of possibilities.
Admire her from afar.

If you come close protect your heart.
It's easy to fall in love with her and she knows that you will but be careful because her love she will never really give.

She can hold you like only a real woman knows how to hold a real man and you will think of her again and again.
At night when the moon dances with the stars she will love you in a way that makes you forget who you are.
But talk to your heart and tell it to remind your soul
that she will walk away and she will never tell you
why she had to go.

Enjoy her but do not fall in love with her because she is elusive like the wind and once she blows out of your life you will long for her to blow back in again and again.

If Only

If only I had answered when you called, if only I had.
If only I had known that you needed me so bad.
If only I had answered when I heard you calling out to me.
I would give anything to have you call on me again.
I swear if you knocked on my heart one more time
I would let you in.
You knocked before and I didn't answer the door.
I had my heart safely locked away and I was
so determined that it would stay.

If only I had taken a moment and dried
just one of your tears.
I didn't know that you really needed me all of these years.
I thought you wanted something from me and
all you really wanted was to give me your love.
I thought you wanted to break my heart and
all you wanted was for us never ever part.
If only I had answered your knock.
If only I had let you in.
I would give anything just to have you knock on my heart again.

If only I had known then what I know now.
I hope, thru the years, you will need me again somehow.
You only wanted to love me and have my love in return.
If only I had known that you wanted me for a lifetime.
If only I could have seen what was in your heart and mind.
If only I had answered, I really wish I had.
If only I had known that you needed me so bad.

I Wish I Knew How To Let You Go

I wish I knew how to let you go in a way where it would not hurt me so.
I wish I knew how to say good-by in a way where it would not make me cry.
I wish I knew how to sleep at night without tossing and turning because you are out of my life.

I wish I knew how to move on and accept the fact that you are really, really gone.
I wish I knew how not to cry.
I wish I had the magic formula for drying my eyes.
I wish that ten years had already past because they tell me that once time goes by the hurt does not last.

I wish I had Aladdin's lamp.
I would make a wish that I was already over you.
I wish I had those magic slippers.
I would click my heels three times and never remember
that your love use to be mine.

I wish I had the luck of the Leprecun, and all things
went my way.
I would wish on green flowing waters that I don't remember you today.
I wish that I had never met you. Then I would not know the pain of trying to forget you.

Spend My Birthday With Me

Would you like to spend my birthday with me?
I have plans that include you, don't you see?
Would you like to spend my birthday with me?
I have champagne chilling and I have got an
awesome feeling that you are the man
I want to spend my birthday with.

Would you like to spend my birthday with me?
I have got definite plans,
but to carry them out I need a hell of a man!
I have got candles burning and
I have really got a yearning.

Would you like to spend my birthday with me?
I have got things on my mind.
Take the phone off the hook and pull the blinds.
All I need is you.
Got this slick black negligee to ease into.
I am another year older and another year wiser too.
Wise enough to know that
I want to spend my birthday with you.

LOVE WON!
LOVE LOST!
LOVE LONGED FOR!

By Verna Buchanan

A very special thanks to those who see the possibilities.
I have over 4,000 writings, lyrics, and poems
across vast subject matters.
To learn more about the author's work and appearances,
you may find information at www.youneedwords.com
Your thoughts and comments are welcomed!
Visit
www.youtube.com/youneedwords
Subscribe to channel it will be updated often.
Submit a like Share link when you visit
the YouTube channel above.

If you need lyrics or a special writings contact us